It's fun to draw

Dogs, Cats,

and Other Animals

It's fun to draw

Dogs, Cats,
and Other Animals

Mark Bergin

Sky Pony Press
New York

Author:
Mark Bergin was born in Hastings, England.
He has illustrated an award-winning series and
written over twenty books. He has done many book
designs, layouts, and storyboards in many styles
including cartoon for numerous books, posters, and
adverts. He lives in Bexhill-on-Sea with his wife
and three children.

HOW TO USE THIS BOOK:
Start by following the numbered splats on the left-
hand page. These steps will ask you to add some
lines to your drawing. The new lines are always
drawn in red so you can see how the drawing builds
from step to step. Read the "You can do it!" splats
to learn about drawing and shading techniques you
can use.

Sky Pony Press books may be purchased in bulk at special discounts
for sales promotion, corporate gifts, fund-raising, or educational
purposes. Special editions can also be created to specifications.
For details, contact the Special Sales Department, Sky Pony Press,
307 West 36th Street, 11th Floor, New York, NY 10018 or info@
skyhorsepublishing.com.

Sky Pony® is a registered trademark of Skyhorse Publishing, Inc.®,
a Delaware corporation.

Visit our website at www.skyponypress.com.

10 9 8 7 6 5 4 3 2

This product conforms to CPSIA 2008

Library of Congress Cataloging-in-Publication Data is available on
file

Cover design by Daniel Brount
Cover illustration by Mark Bergin
ISBN: 978-1-5107-4360-1
Printed in the United States of America

Contents

8   Cat

10   Dog

12   Fish

14   Parakeet

16   Guinea pig

18   Horse

20   Lizard

22   Parrot

24   Rabbit

26   Rat

28   Snake

30   Stick insect

32   Spider

34   Tortoise

Contents

36 Zebra
38 Lion
40 Giraffe
42 Ostrich
44 Eagle
46 Wildebeest
48 Elephant
50 Leopard
52 Warthog
54 Thomson's gazelle
56 Crocodile
58 Baboon
60 Hippo
62 Cheetah
64 Index

It's fun to draw

Dogs, Cats,

and other Animals

Cat

1 Start by drawing this shape for the head.

2 Add an ear, nose, eye, mouth, and whiskers.

3 Draw in a bean-shaped body.

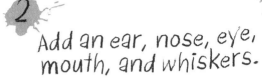

you can do it!

Use a felt-tip marker for the lines and add color using colored pencils.

4 Add two back legs and a belly shape.

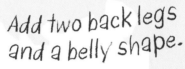

splat-a-fact

Cats sleep for 16-18 hours a day.

5 Draw in two front legs and a tail.

Dog

1 Start with an oval for the head. Add cheeks and eyes.

2 Draw in the ears, and add a bone in the dog's mouth.

you can do it!

Use crayons to add color and a felt-tip marker for the lines.

3 Add an oval for the body.

4 Draw in the back legs and the tail.

splat-a-fact

Dogs have better hearing than humans and can hear sounds at four times the distance.

5 Draw in the front legs, and add a collar.

Fish

1 Start by drawing the body shape.

splat-a-fact
Fish sleep with their eyes open!

2 Add a curved line for the face. Draw in the mouth and a dot for the eye.

3 Add a tail and two fins.

4 Draw in the striped markings.

12

Parakeet

1 Start with the head. Add a beak and a dot for the eye.

2 Add a body and two feet.

3 Draw in the tail feathers.

you can do it!

Use oil pastels and smudge them with your finger. Use a felt-tip marker for the lines.

4

Add the wings.

Guinea pig

you can do it!

Cut out the shapes from colored paper and glue in place. The guinea pig head must overlap the body. Use felt-tip marker for the lines.

1 Start by cutting out a curvy shape for the body. Glue it down.

2 Cut out the head shape with tufts of hair. Glue down.

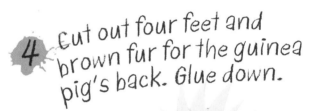

4 Cut out four feet and brown fur for the guinea pig's back. Glue down.

3 Cut out a brown patch for the face. Glue it down. Cut out an ear and glue down. Draw in the eye and nose.

splat-a-fact

A group of guinea pigs is called a herd.

MAKE SURE YOU GET AN ADULT TO HELP YOU WHEN USING SCISSORS!

16

Horse

1 Start by drawing a bean-shaped body.

2 Draw in a neck and a head. Add dots for the eyes and nostrils.

3 Draw in four legs with hooves.

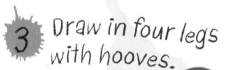

4 Add a tail and a mane. Draw in ears and spots on the body. Add a piece of grass to the mouth.

19

Lizard

1 Start with this shape for the head.

2 Add two circles with dots for the eyes, a mouth, and dots for the nostrils.

you can do it!

Use a pen for the lines then paint with watercolor. Add colored inks to the wet paint for interest.

splat-a-fact

Geckos are the only lizards that have a voice.

3 Draw in a wiggly body shape.

4 Add legs and splayed feet. Draw in markings on the body.

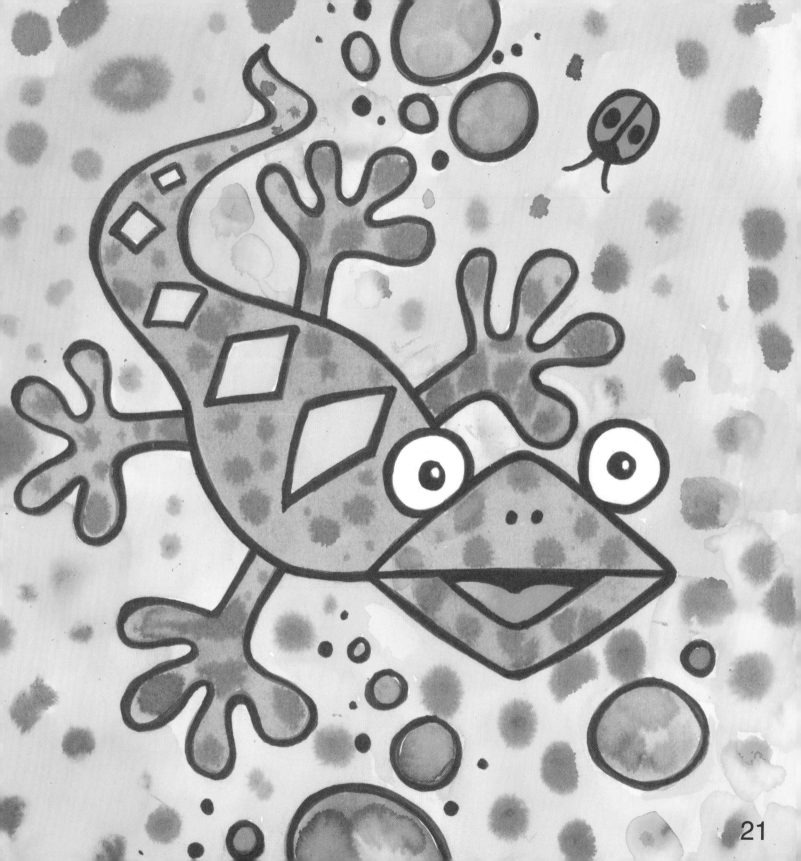

Parrot

1

Start by drawing the head shape. Add a dot for the eye.

2 Add the body and the beak.

3 Draw in the wings and tail feathers.

Splat-a-fact

There are more than 350 different kinds of parrots.

4 Add the feet and perch.

5 Draw in the feathers.

You can do it!

Add color with watercolor paint. Use felt-tip markers for the lines.

Rabbit

1 Start by drawing a circle for the head.

2 Add ears.

you can do it!
Use oil pastels and smudge them with your finger. Use a felt-tip marker for the lines.

3 Draw in the eyes, nose, mouth, teeth, and whiskers.

4 Add a rounded body and two back feet.

5 Draw in the front legs and paws.

24

25

Rat

1 Start with the head shape. Add a dot for the eye.

2 Draw in two ears, a nose, mouth, and whiskers.

3 Draw in the body.

4 Draw in the two back legs.

5 Draw in the front legs and a tail. Add toes to each foot.

you can do it!
Draw the lines with a felt-tip marker and then add color with watercolor paint.

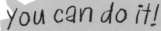

26

Snake

1 Start by drawing this head shape.

2 Add dots for the eyes and nostrils.

splat-a-fact
Snakes belong to the animal group called reptiles.

3 Draw in the mouth, and add a forked tongue.

4 Draw a long, curving body.

you can do it!
Draw the lines with a felt-tip marker and use torn tissue paper for color.

5 Add a diamond-shaped pattern.

stick insect

1 Start with the head shape. Add dots for eyes.

2 Add two antennae and pincer shapes under the head.

3 Draw in the stick insect's body.

splat-a-fact
Stick insect eggs can take up to 2 years to hatch.

4 Add three legs and feet to each side.

spider

1. Start by drawing two overlapping circles for the head and body.

2. Add four dots for the eyes and two fangs.

3. Draw in three legs on each side.

you can do it!
Color the picture with crayons. First place different textured surfaces under the paper to create interesting effects.

4. Add two more front legs.

32

Tortoise

you can do it!
Color in with watercolor paint. Use a felt-tip marker for the lines.

1 Start with an oval shape for the shell.

2 Add a pattern to the shell. Draw in another curved line around the shell's base.

3 Draw in the head, and add an eye, mouth, and nostrils.

4 Add four legs and a pointed tail.

splat-a-fact
Tortoises have a protective shell around their body.

Zebra

1 Start with the head and a dot for the eye.

2 Add ears, mouth, nostrils, and hair.

3 Draw in the neck to a bean-shaped body.

4 Add the mane and the tail.

5 Draw four legs and hooves.

you can do it!
Use wax crayons for background texture painted over with watercolor paint. Use black felt-tip marker for the zebra's stripes.

splat-a-fact
No two zebra stripes are exactly the same.

Lion

1 Start with the head and add two dots for the eyes.

2 Add the nose, mouth, and whiskers and draw in the mane.

splat-a-fact
Lions rest for about 20 hours each day.

3 Add the body with a curly tail and four legs with big paws.

39

Giraffe

1 Start with the head, mouth, hair, and dots for the eyes and nostrils.

2 Draw two long lines for the neck and an oval shape for the body.

3 Add a mane, two ears, and tufts on the horns.

you can do it!

Use wax crayons for texture, painted over with water color paint. Use brown ink for the giraffe pattern and a felt-tip marker for the lines.

Splat-a-fact
Giraffes are the tallest animals on earth.

4 Draw in four legs and a tail.

Ostrich

1 Start with the head, adding a beak and a dot for the eye.

2 Draw two lines for the neck.

3 Draw an oval shape with a flat bottom for the body. Add a line at the front and the wing.

4 Add two legs with clawed feet and big tail feathers.

you can do it!
Use oil pastels, and use your finger to smudge them. Use a felt-tip marker for the lines.

42

Eagle

1 Start with the head and the body.

2 Add an eye, a beak, two feet, and tail feathers.

you can do it!
Use wax crayons for the feather shapes and textures. Paint over with watercolor paint. Use a felt-tip marker for the lines.

3 Draw two wings.

splat-a-fact
Eagles have excellent eyesight and razor-sharp talons.

4 Add the wing feathers.

44

Wildebeest

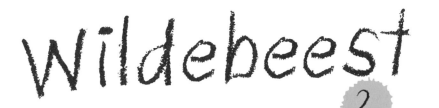

1 Start with the head and the horns.

2 Add two ears and dots for the eyes and nostrils.

splat-a fact
A wildebeest is also called a gnu (noo).

you can do it!
Add color with watercolor paint and use a sponge to dab more color on for added texture. Use a felt-tip marker for the lines.

3 Draw the body shape and neck.

4 Add four legs and a tail.

Elephant

1 Start by cutting out the shape of the head.

2 Cut out the tusk and add a dot for an eye.

3 Cut an oval for the body.

splat-a-fact
An elephant is the only mammal that cannot jump.

MAKE SURE YOU GET AN ADULT TO HELP YOU WHEN USING SCISSORS!

4 Cut out the tip of the tail, four legs, and draw in the toenails.

Leopard

you can do it!
Use colored pencils and felt-tip markers for the lines. Use both for the leopard's spots.

1 Start with the head.

2 Add ears, nose, mouth, and a dot for an eye.

3 Draw in the neck and the body.

4 Add whiskers and a tail.

splat-a-fact

Leopards are great climbers and like to eat and sleep in trees.

5 Draw in four legs and paws.

50

Warthog

1 Start with the head and a dot for the eye.

2 Draw in neck, hair, tusks, and ears.

3 Draw the body shape.

you can do it!
Use a dark pencil for the outline and add color with watercolor paint.

4 Add four legs, a tail, and two dots for nostrils.

Thomson's gazelle

1 Start with the head and add a dot for the eye.

2 Draw two horns, ears, a nose, and the cheek marking.

3 Add the neck.

4 Draw an oval shaped body, a tail, and body markings.

you can do it!
Use colored pastel pencils and smudge the colors with your finger. Draw the outline with a felt-tip marker.

Splat-a-fact
A Thompson's gazelle has excellent sight, hearing and sense of smell.

5 Add the tail and black-tipped four legs.

Crocodile

1 Start with the head.

2 Add a nostril, eye, teeth, and two small bumps.

3 Draw two lines for the body and tail and a line for its belly.

you can do it!
Use colored inks and a felt-tip marker for the lines.

4 Add four legs, spikes on its back, lines across its belly and above the eye.

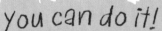

56

Baboon

1 Start with the head and chest.

2 Add the body and lots of fur.

3 Draw in the tail, one ear, and dots for eyes and nostrils.

you can do it!
Use wax crayons for texture and paint over it with watercolor paint. Use a felt-tip marker for the lines.

4 Add two front legs and two back legs.

58

Hippo

You can do it!
Color in with watercolor paint. Use a felt-tip marker for the lines.

1 Start with the head and two dots for the eyes.

2 Add two ears and a mouth.

3 Draw a big oval body.

4 Add a tail and four legs with toenails.

Splat-a-fact
Hippos spend most of the day in water but they do not swim.

Cheetah

1 Start with a head.

2 Add a dot for the eye and the mouth.

3 Add a long oval shape for the body, two lines for the neck, and a dot for the nose.

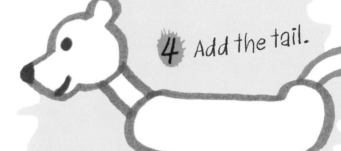

you can do it!

Draw the outlines with a brown felt-tip marker. Color in with colored pencils.

4 Add the tail.

5 Add four legs.

Index

B
Baboon 58-59

C
cat 8-9
cheetah 62-63
crayon 10, 18, 30, 32, 38, 40, 44, 58
crocodile 56-57

D
dog 10-11

E
eagle 44-45
elephant 48-49

F
felt-tip marker 8, 10, 12, 14, 16, 18, 20, 22, 24, 26, 28, 30, 38, 40, 42, 44, 46, 48, 50, 54, 56, 58, 60, 62
fish 12-13

G
giraffe 40-41
guinea pig 16-17

H
hippo 60-61
horse 18-19

L
leopard 22-23
lion 10-11
lizard 20-21

O
ostrich 42-43

P
paint 18, 20, 24, 26, 30, 34, 40, 44, 46, 52, 58, 60
paper 16, 28
parakeet 14-15
parrot 22-23
pastels 14, 24, 42, 54
pencils 22, 24, 26, 34

R
rabbit 24-25
rat 26-27

S
smudging 14, 24, 42, 54
snake 28-29
spider 32-33
sponge 46
stick insect 30-31

T
Thomson's gazelle 54-55
tortoise 34-35

W
warthog 52-53
wildebeest 46-47

Z
zebra 36-37